THE
DINOSAUR
WORLD

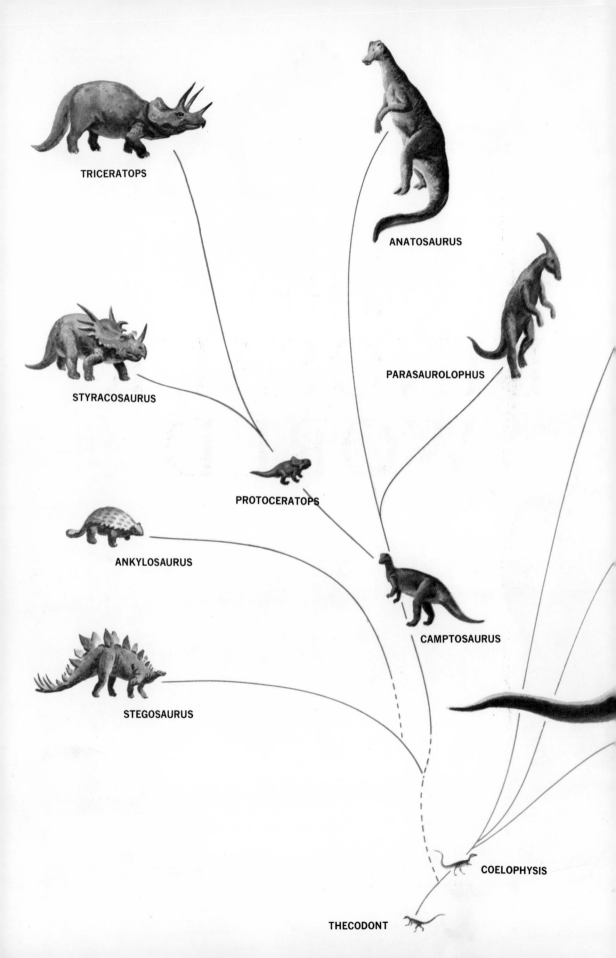

TRICERATOPS

ANATOSAURUS

STYRACOSAURUS

PARASAUROLOPHUS

PROTOCERATOPS

ANKYLOSAURUS

CAMPTOSAURUS

STEGOSAURUS

COELOPHYSIS

THECODONT

ORNITHOMIMUS

TYRANNOSAURUS

THE
DINOSAUR
WORLD

By
Edwin H. Colbert, Ph.D., Sc.D.

Curator of Vertebrate Paleontology
The Museum of Northern Arizona

Curator Emeritus
The American Museum of Natural History

Professor Emeritus
Columbia University

Illustrated by
George Geygan
and
Paul Geygan

BRONTOSAURUS

Stravon Educational Press
New York, N. Y.

Some of the material in this book originally appeared under the title *The World of Dinosaurs* copyright ©1961, by Edwin H. Colbert.

Library of Congress Cataloging in Publication Data

Colbert, Edwin Harris, 1905–
The dinosaur world.

Includes Index.

SUMMARY: Examines all known dinosaurs including discussions of their characteristics and classification and the collection and study of bones and fossils.

1. Dinosauria – Juvenile literature.   1. Dinosaurs   I. Geygan, George.
II. Geygan, Paul.   III. Title.   QE862 . D5C66   568' . 19   76-16586
ISBN 0-87396-081-5

Printed in the United States of America

CONTENTS

INTRODUCTION

Many **millions of years ago,** when the world was very different from the world in which we live, there were dinosaurs on the land. They inhabited the continents, they were numerous, and they were of many kinds. Some of them were giants like *Brontosaurus,* others were rather small like *Ornitholestes,* a contemporary of *Brontosaurus* .

The dinosaurs were reptiles, related to modern crocodiles and alligators. They lived during the Mesozoic era of earth history (*see* the geologic time chart on page 60). The first dinosaurs appeared in the latter part of the Triassic period, about 185 million years ago. From them the later dinosaurs developed along many varied lines of evolution during the Jurassic and Cretaceous periods, and became extinct at the end of Cretaceous times, about sixty-five million years ago. It is evident therefore, that the dinosaurs lived through a span of something more than 100 million years, which represents in time about a fifth of the known fossil record. The dinosaurs were indeed very successful animals.

It is often said that the dinosaurs were failures, because they are now extinct. How can we make such a judgment? How sure can we be that our descendants will be on the earth 100 million years from now?

However one may wish to look at the dinosaurs, they are definitely well known — all over the world. And yet less than a century and a half ago the former presence of dinosaurs on the earth was completely unrealized by our nineteenth century ancestors. Of course it is quite probable that dinosaur bones had been discovered by many people through time. Moreover, it is quite possible that the legends of giants, so prevalent throughout much of human history, were based in part upon the discoveries of dinosaur bones. But the recognition of dinosaur bones for what they are — the remains of prehistoric reptiles — did not come until the third decade of the nineteenth century, when two Englishmen, a physician named Gideon Mantell and a clergyman named William Buckland, separately described dinosaur bones that had been discovered in southern England. Even then these fossils were not called di-

8

BRONTOSAURUS

nosaurs; they were simply regarded as the remains of large, extinct reptiles.

The idea of dinosaurs as distinctive reptiles, quite different from any reptiles living today, was suggested in 1842 by Sir Richard Owen the great English anatomist. In the Proceedings of the British Association for the Advancement of Science, published in that year, Owen said that "The combination of such characters. . . .will, it is presumed, be deemed sufficient ground for establishing a distinct tribe or suborder of Saurian Reptiles, for which I would propose the name of *Dinosauria.*" (This name is formed from the combination of two Greek roots; *dinos* meaning terrible, and *sauros* meaning lizard.) Thus the terrible lizards, or more properly the terrible reptiles, came into the consciousness of Man. And so greatly has our knowledge of dinosaurs been expanded and extended, that today these ancient reptiles are universally known, and the word *dinosaur* has become a common noun in languages all over the world.

ORNITHOLESTES

SKELETON IN THE ROCK

FOSSILS OF DINOSAURS

What we know about dinosaurs is based upon the study of *fossils* of these ancient reptiles, preserved in the rocks of the earth's crust. The study of fossils is the science of *paleontology.* Fossils are the records of prehistoric life. They are the remains or indications of animals and plants, now extinct, contained within sands and sandstones, muds and shales, marls and limestones, these being *sediments* deposited by water in rivers, lakes and seas, and by wind on the land. Fossils are commonly the hard parts of organisms, such as wood or shell or bone, that have been petrified or transformed into stone. The transformation of wood or shell or bone into stone may progress through various stages. Sometimes the hard parts of an animal or plant are preserved in their original condition. If, however, the fossil is of any considerable geologic age, the hard parts usually are infiltrated or replaced by mineral matter. If the small internal cavities of wood, shell or bone are filled with

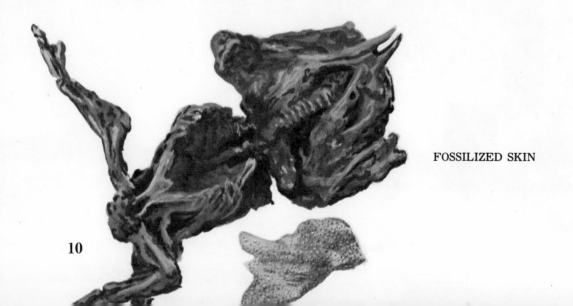

FOSSILIZED SKIN

10

minerals deposited from ground waters the fossil is *per-mineralized.* If the process has continued so that the hard parts are *replaced* by minerals the fossil is completely *petrified.* Yet although petrified, the fossil generally preserves the texture and the microscopic structure of the original wood, shell or bone.

Occasionally even the soft parts of animals or plants may be fossilized. Fossils also may be secondary evidence of ancient life, such as footprints or nests or eggs. Fossils occur in many forms.

The fossil remains of dinosaurs usually are found as fragments of bones or teeth in the rocks. Once in a while a skeleton or a part of a skeleton is discovered, but such finds are not common and usually result from long hours of diligent exploration in the field by experienced *paleontologists,* the students of ancient life.

A few dinosaur mummies may be seen in some museums. These are the fossilized carcasses of dinosaurs in which the texture of the skin is clearly preserved. Fossil dinosaur eggs are known from various parts of the world. Perhaps the most spectacular of such discoveries are nests of clusters of eggs belonging to the little Cretaceous dinosaur *Protoceratops,* from Mongolia. The *Protoceratops* eggs, about eight inches in length, are elongated as are the eggs of some modern lizards, and their surfaces are marked by little ridges. Other dinosaur eggs found in Cretaceous beds in southern France are round, as large as very large grapefruit, and have pebbly surfaces. It would seem that these eggs were laid by large brontosaur-like dinosaurs, named *Hypselosaurus.* Dinosaur eggs also have been found in Montana, in Portugal, in Tanzania, Africa, and in Brazil.

Footprints and trackways made by dinosaurs are rather common in rocks of Mesozoic age. In recent years a spectacular rock surface displaying thousands of Triassic dinosaur footprints has been uncovered at Rocky Hill, Connecticut, not far from New Haven. Here one can see trackways made by numerous primitive dinosaurs of various sizes that crossed and recrossed an ancient mud-flat bordering a river or perhaps a little lake. In fact, some of the trackways lead from the mud-flat into what was once shallow water, as indicated by fossil ripple marks across which the dinosaur footprints are impressed. Huge brontosaur tracks from central Texas make a graphic display of how these giant reptiles once walked ponderously through soft mud at the edge of an ancient sea. And in western Australia the trackways of gigantic meat-eating dinosaurs are preserved in rocks of Cretaceous age, now along the shore of the Indian Ocean and exposed to view only at low tide. These are but a few examples; dinosaur footprints are of world-wide occurrence.

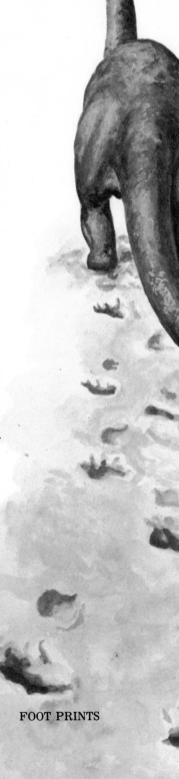

EGGS   FOOT PRINTS

COLLECTING AND STUDYING DINOSAURS

What we have learned about dinosaurs to date is the result of many studies of their fossils, made by paleontologists throughout the world during the past 150 years. But in order to study dinosaurs and to understand them, it is necessary to collect their fossils in the field, and to bring them to the museum where they can be cleaned and properly preserved.

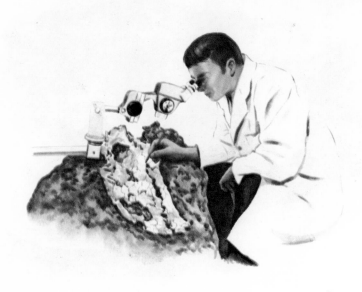

It requires a great deal of knowledge and training, of skill and persistence, to collect dinosaurs. Special methods, developed by many paleontologists through more than a century of experience, are used to expose the bones in the rock, to harden them, and to protect them against breakage, so that they can be removed to the laboratory.

After the fossils are discovered (usually by finding a fragment of bone protruding from a cliff or a bank) they are uncovered with picks and shovels, small tools and brushes. Fossil bones are hardened by the application of thin, white shellac or some other solution, after which they are encased in burlap and plaster of Paris bandages in much the same fashion that a broken limb is immobilized by a physician. Thus the fossils, which otherwise would disintegrate, can be shipped to the laboratory.

In the laboratory the plaster casts are removed, the fossils are carefully cleaned and further hardened. Missing parts may be restored in plaster.

Then they are ready to be studied. They are compared with other fossils and with published descriptions of fossils. Finally, when the fossils have been identified and interpreted they may be placed in an exhibition hall—if they are worthy of a display.

DEFINITION OF THE DINOSAURS

What were the dinosaurs? As we have said, they were reptiles of varied size and form that lived during Mesozoic times. The reptiles, represented in our modern world by the lizards and snakes, turtles, crocodiles and alligators, and by the tuatara — a little lizard-like reptile living in New Zealand — are often designated as being "cold-blooded," backboned animals. Modern reptiles have no internal method of regulating the body temperature, as do the "warm-blooded" animals like ourselves. Thus the body temperatures in the reptiles as we know them fluctuate up and down more or less as the temperatures of their environments change. On cold days a reptile will be sluggish because of its low body temperature; on hot days a reptile will be active, with a high body temperature. But reptiles

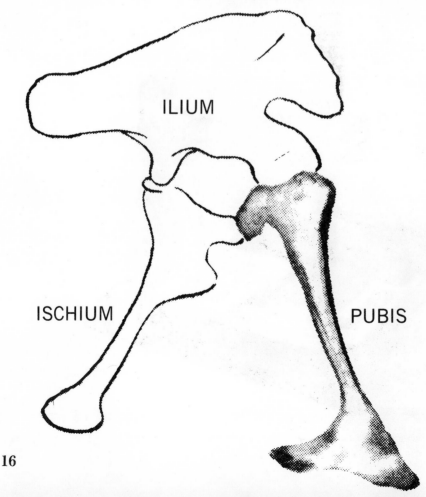

ILIUM

ISCHIUM

PUBIS

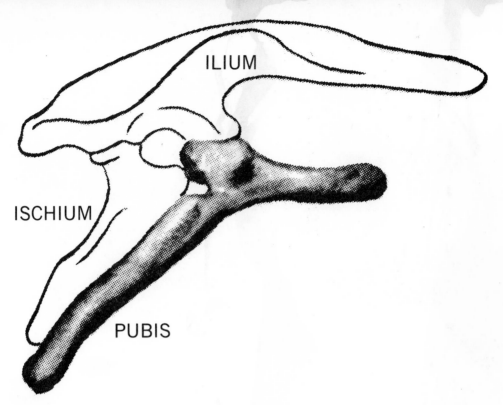

ILIUM

ISCHIUM

PUBIS

cannot withstand extreme or even moderately low temperatures, and likewise they cannot withstand very high temperatures. They must seek protection underground or in the shade or in water.

It is reasonable to assume that the dinosaurs were similar to modern reptiles, especially their crocodilian cousins, in their tolerances to temperatures. But some students think that perhaps the dinosaurs were independently "warm-blooded," and that this may explain in part their long success. We will never know for sure.

It should be mentioned here that the dinosaurs cannot be defined upon the basis of size. It is a common mistake to think that all dinosaurs were giants. A majority of them were giants, but there were medium-sized and even small dinosaurs. It is necessary to define the dinosaurs within the world of reptiles by their anatomical structure, as revealed for the most part by their fossil bones. Careful studies, based upon this evidence, show that the dinosaurs cannot be placed within a single group of reptiles, but rather that they belong to two separate reptilian *orders,* as distinct from each other as modern horses and rhinoceroses on the one hand are distinct from modern deer and cattle on the other.

SAURISCHIAN SKULL

The two orders of dinosaurs are the *Saurischia* and the *Ornithischia*. These two groups of dinosaurs had their origin within a common ancestry before late Triassic times, and from this same ancestry there arose the crocodilians, and the pterosaurs or flying reptiles.

In the saurischian dinosaurs the three bones of the pelvis, as seen in a side view, are arranged with the *ilium* at the top to form a strong connection between the hip girdle and the vertebrae or "backbone," with the *ischium* beneath pointed toward the rear, and with the *pubis* also beneath, pointed forwardly. These two lower bones afford strong attachment for muscles to the legs and to the tail. Such an arrangement of pelvic bones is found in many other reptiles.

In the ornithischian dinosaurs the *pubis* has in effect rotated back so that it is parallel to and pressed against the *ischium*, an arrangement similar to that seen in modern birds. Moreover, there is a long, forwardly directed process on the *ilium*, and another one below it on the *pubis*, these reflecting special muscular developments.

The saurischian skull, with two large openings on each side behind the eye for the accommodation of bulging jaw muscles, and with other openings in front of the eye, seemingly to reduce the weight of the structure, is furnished with teeth that occupy the margins of the jaws, in front and along their sides. If there is any reduction in the teeth it takes place on the sides of the jaws.

The ornithischian skull, in which the openings behind and in front of the eyes may be much reduced or variously eliminated, has the teeth confined to the sides of the jaws. In some of the ornithischian dinosaurs these teeth are greatly increased in numbers to form complex grinding mills. The fronts of the jaws are toothless and form a bird-like beak that in life had a horny covering. An extra bone covers the front of the lower jaws, and in some ornithischians there is an opposing extra bone on the front of the skull.

There are many other differences between the saurischian and ornithischian dinosaurs throughout the skull and skeleton. However, the basic differences in the skull, teeth and pelvis indicate how widely the two orders of dinosaurs diverged from each other.

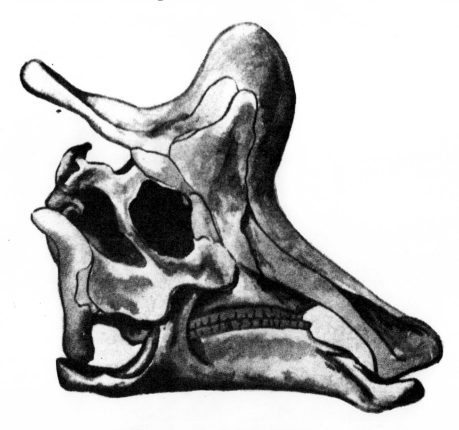

ORNITHISCHIAN SKULL

CLASSIFICATION OF THE DINOSAURS

The dinosaurs were numerous and various during their long Mesozoic reign. Therefore they may be subdivided within the two orders, the Saurischia and Ornithischia, into several suborders and a considerable number of families, according to their resemblances and differences. The suborders of dinosaurs are as follows.

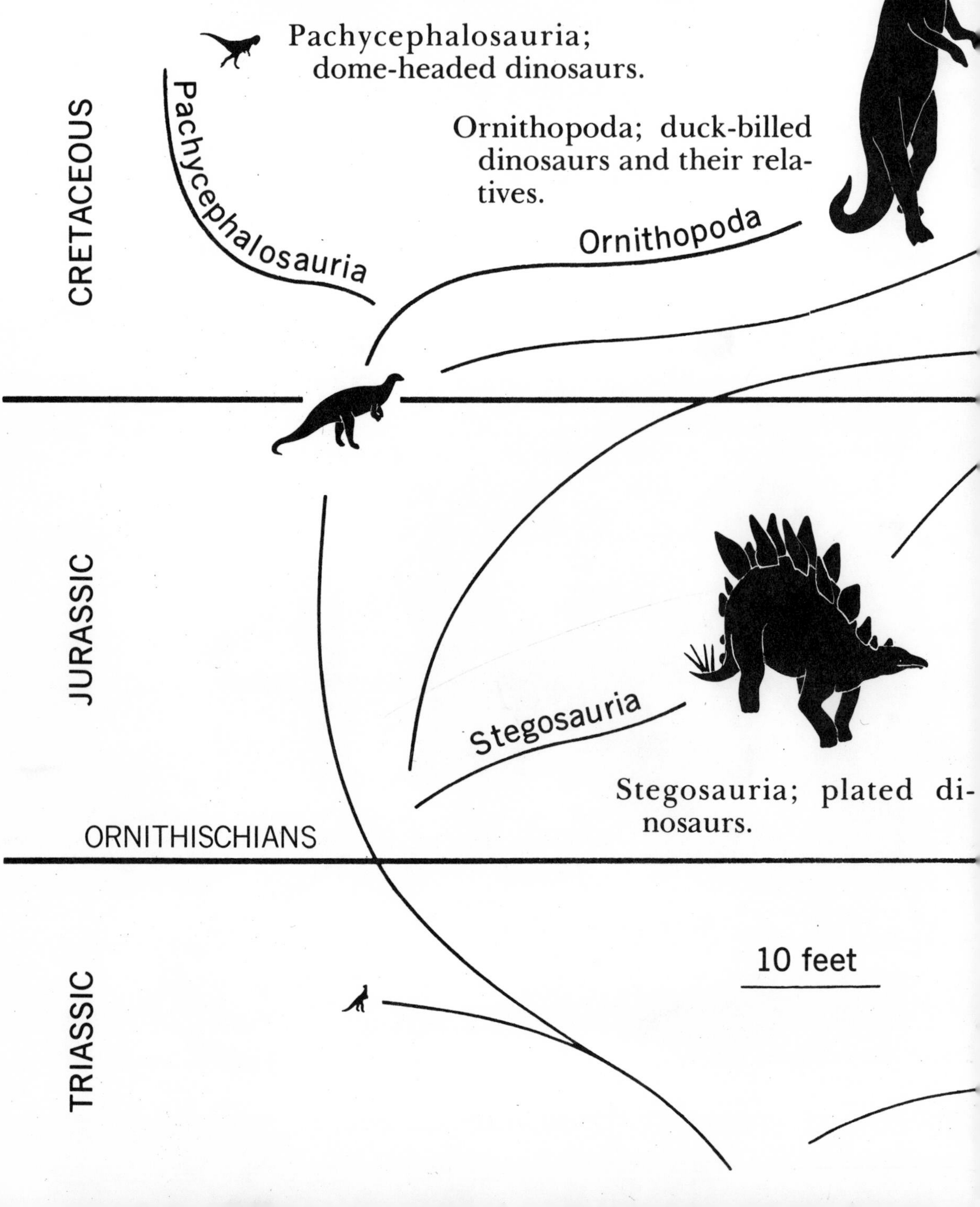

Pachycephalosauria; dome-headed dinosaurs.

Ornithopoda; duck-billed dinosaurs and their relatives.

Ornithopoda

Pachycephalosauria

CRETACEOUS

Stegosauria

Stegosauria; plated dinosaurs.

JURASSIC

ORNITHISCHIANS

10 feet

TRIASSIC

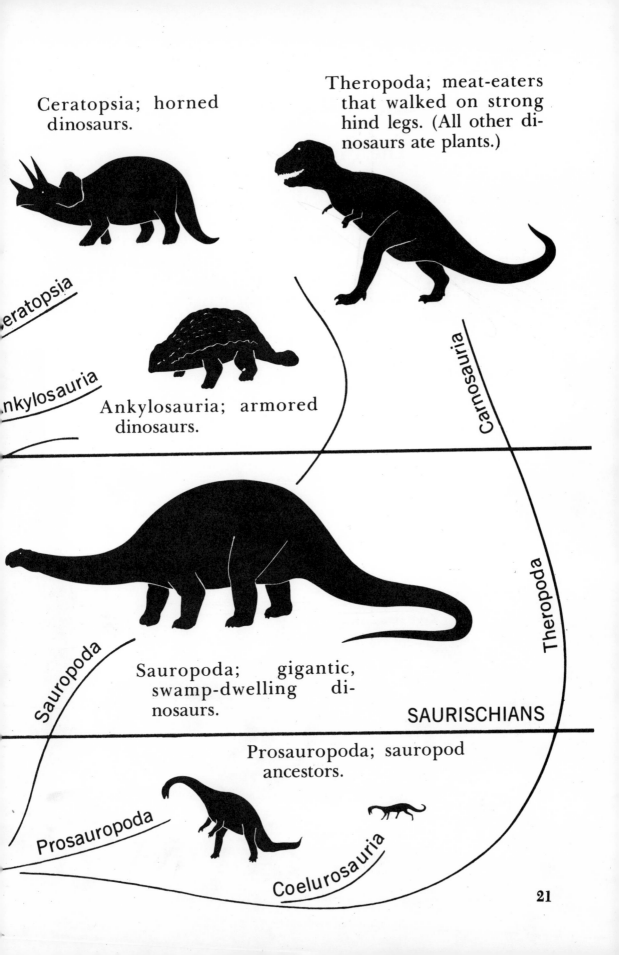

Ceratopsia; horned dinosaurs.

Theropoda; meat-eaters that walked on strong hind legs. (All other dinosaurs ate plants.)

Ceratopsia

Carnosauria

Ankylosauria

Ankylosauria; armored dinosaurs.

Sauropoda

Theropoda

Sauropoda; gigantic, swamp-dwelling dinosaurs.

SAURISCHIANS

Prosauropoda; sauropod ancestors.

Prosauropoda

Coelurosauria

21

SAURISCHIAN DINOSAURS

The First Saurischians

One of the earliest dinosaurs is the theropod *Coelophysis*, pictured at the bottom of this page. It is known from numerous fossils found in New Mexico. The skeleton of this small Triassic theropod is graceful, and delicately constructed, with hollow bones. It is about seven or eight feet in length, and since much of this length is taken up by the long, slender neck and the correspondingly long tail, the skeleton gives the impression of a very slender, light reptile, perhaps weighing no more than seventy-five pounds. In life *Coelophysis* must have been a quick, agile animal, an active hunter that pursued and caught small reptiles in the undergrowth of ancient, tropical forests. *Coelophysis* walked on strong, bird-like hind legs, as did

COELOPHYSIS

PAUL GEYGAN

other early dinosaurs, and the small front limbs, having hands armed with sharp claws, were used for grasping, digging and scratching. The long jaws of *Coelophysis* are set with sharp, blade-like teeth.

Among the skeletons of *Coelophysis* found in New Mexico are two containing the bones of very small *Coelophysis* individuals. Are these the bones of unborn reptiles? Probably not, because even though small, they seem too large and well formed to have been embryos. More likely these are the remains of unfortunate youngsters, eaten by cannibalistic adults. We know that cannibalism is not uncommon among modern reptiles.

In recent years a dinosaur very closely related to *Coelophysis* has been discovered in Rhodesia, Africa. This dinosaur, named *Syntarsus,* indicates that in late Triassic time the continents were so connected that the early dinosaurs could range widely across the face of the earth.

Coelophysis and *Syntarsus* belong to a subdivision of theropod dinosaurs known as the Coelurosauria. The coelurosaurs, which persisted from the Triassic until the end of the Cretaceous period, were all comparatively small, lightly constructed theropods.

Small Hunters

The history of the dinosaurs is in general a story of giants. But there are exceptions, among the most notable of which are the coelurosaurs.

During late Jurassic time, the coelurosaur *Ornitholestes*, shown on page 9, inhabited a landscape dominated by giants. This little theropod, no more than six feet in length, continued the anatomical features and the mode of life so typical of its Triassic ancestors. It was a hunter of small game, perhaps preying largely on the early lizards with which it was contemporaneous.

Compsognathus, found in the upper Jurassic beds of central Europe is one of the smallest dinosaurs known. It is no larger than a good-sized chicken.

Running Theropods

Among the late Cretaceous dinosaurs the coelurosaur *Ornithomimus* carried on, with certain changes, the features so characteristic of its early theropod ancestors. The skeleton of this theropod dinosaur is lightly built and graceful, even though it is about equal to a modern ostrich in size. The long hind limbs show that this dinosaur was able to run with great speed across wide plains, either in pursuit of its prey or to escape from its enemies. The slender front limbs were admirably fitted for reaching into low trees for fruit, or for digging in the ground for roots and insects. The small skull, carried on a long, flexible neck, is completely devoid of teeth; the jaws in life probably had a horny covering, like the beak of a bird. This dinosaur has been found in North America and in Asia.

ORNITHOMIMUS

Giant Hunters

Since time immemorial there have been the hunted and the hunters; the animals that get their energy from eating plants, and the animals that feed upon the plant-eaters. During the Jurassic and Cretaceous periods the roles of hunted and hunters were enacted on a titanic scale by the dinosaurs; the hunted being varied plant-eating dinosaurs and the hunters being those theropods (most of which were giants) known as Carnosauria. *Allosaurus,* the skeleton of which is about thirty-five feet in length, was a carnosaur of Jurassic age that probably preyed upon other dinosaurs, including *Stegosaurus,* an ornithischian dinosaur and a contemporary of *Allosaurus.*

Allosaurus walked on strong hind legs, as did all of the meat-eating dinosaurs. The front limbs are relatively

ALLOSAURUS

small, but the large claws on the fingers indicate that the hands were none the less useful for grasping and for clawing. The skull in this dinosaur is very large, which in life increased the gape of the jaws and the power of their bite. And the jaws are set with blade-like teeth, the edges of which are serrated, like the blade of a steak knife. In late Jurassic times *Allosaurus* was the arch-predator of the North American continent, just as the lion and the tiger are today in the wilds of Africa and of Asia.

Allosaurus is typical of the giant carnosaurs that roamed the continents in Jurassic times. The differences between the carnosaurs at this stage of earth history were differences in details. Thus *Ceratosaurus,* which shared the late Jurassic scene in North America with *Allosaurus* was a large carnosaur with a horn on its nose. *Megalosaurus,* in Europe and incidentally one of the first dinosaurs to be described, was essentially similar to *Allosaurus.*

Predatory animals commonly are less varied than the animals on which they prey. For example there are numerous kinds of antelopes in Africa today, but they are preyed upon by only a few types of predators. Lions, leopards and cheetahs are the cats that hunt big game. Hyenas also prey upon large antelopes as do the hunting dogs of Africa. Jackals follow the large hunters to eat the left-overs. And so it was in Jurassic times among the dinosaurs.

The specializations for hunting and for killing, so highly developed in *Allosaurus,* were carried to an extreme in *Gorgosaurus* and *Tyrannosaurus,* among the last of the dinosaurs that lived in North America near the end of Cretaceous times. *Tyrannosaurus* was the giant among carnivorous dinosaurs; the skeleton is about fifty feet in length and stands some twenty feet high. Indeed, *Tyrannosaurus* was the largest carnivorous animal ever to walk on land.

Its skull is of a huge size, thus giving remarkable power to the jaws of this great reptile, and these jaws are armed with very large, dagger-like teeth. Evidently the power of destruction was concentrated in the jaws, for the front limbs of *Tyrannosaurus* are ridiculously small and could not have been of much use to aid in catching and holding prey.

The duck-billed dinosaurs, of which *Anatosaurus* (or *"Trachodon"*) was a contemporary of *Tyrannosaurus*, may have been among the victims of this giant hunter.

A close relative of *Tyrannosaurus,* named *Tarbosaurus,* lived in Asia during late Cretaceous time. And living with *Tarbosaurus* was a truly gigantic carnosaur, *Deinocheirus,* unfortunately known at the present time only from its huge forelimbs.

TYRANNOSAURUS

ANATOSAURUS

Deinonychosaurs

A third subdivision of the theropod dinosaurs is that of the Deinonychosauria. The deinonychosaurs are of medium or even of rather small size. One medium-sized member of the group, *Deinonychus,* of early Cretaceous age deserves mention because of its unusual specializations. The skull of *Deinonychus* looks very much like the skulls of other carnosaurs. But the feet are most unusual. The hind foot has an extremely large claw on the inner toe. It would seem that this dinosaur walked and ran on two toes of each hind foot, the large inner claw being held up out of the way. This huge claw would seem to have been specialized for tearing and cutting. The claws of the front feet are also very large. And what is especially surprising is the struc-

DEINONYCHUS

ture of the tail, in which the vertebrae are bound together in such a way that the tail must have been very rigid. One may picture *Deinonychus* as seizing and holding its prey with the large clawed forefeet and ripping the unfortunate victim with the scimitar-like claws of the hind feet. Perhaps the rigid tail helped to stabilize the body during the struggles of predation.

PAUL GEYGAN

Sauropod Ancestors

We now come to the giants among giants, the sauropod dinosaurs and their ancestors, the Triassic prosauropods. In late Triassic time the prosauropods appeared as the largest of Triassic dinosaurs. They are well exemplified by *Plateosaurus*, known from several fine skeletons found in southern Germany, a reptile twenty feet or more in length. The heavy leg bones, the enlargement of the front limbs, the long neck and the closely-set, leaf-shaped teeth show

PLATEOSAURUS

that this dinosaur was diverging from the primitive theropod type (as typified by *Coelophysis*) and developing in the direction of the giant, swamp-dwelling sauropods of later Mesozoic times. *Plateosaurus* was probably a slow, inoffensive dinosaur that fed upon a variety of animals and plants.

Prosauropods lived widely across the late Triassic continents. *Anchisaurus* was an inhabitant of North America, *Herrerasaurus* of South America, *Lufengosaurus* of Asia and *Plateosauravus* of Africa — all very similar to *Plateosaurus*. Such were the beginnings of a long line of giants.

PAUL GEYGAN

DIPLODOCUS

The Great Sauropods

The evolutionary trends that began in the Triassic pro-sauropods reached their climax in the greatest of the dinosaurs, the gigantic sauropods, the largest of all land animals. The sauropods lived throughout the world during Jurassic and Cretaceous times.

The legs on these dinosaurs are very heavy to support great weights, frequently ranging from 20 to 40 tons. The vertebrae are complex, to form an interlocking, flexible but powerful beam, the center support of the body. The neck and the tail are long, and the comparatively small skull usually has elevated nostrils. The structure of the skull and skeleton indicate that perhaps these dinosaurs spent much time wading in water, probably in lakes and swamps, and feeding upon soft plants.

Diplodocus, above, is a slender sauropod, the skeleton of which is almost ninety feet in length.

Brachiosaurus, on the right, though shorter, is the most massive of these dinosaurs, having a probable live weight of more than 80 tons, and is peculiar in having very long fore limbs and high shoulders. Both of these sauropods, of late Jurassic age, are found in North America, and *Brachiosaurus* is also found in Africa. *Brontosaurus,* seen on pages 8 and 9 is another well-known Jurassic sauropod. The sauropods are all generally similar.

BRACHIOSAURUS

ORNITHISCHIAN DINOSAURS

The First Ornithischians

Until a few years ago no ornithischian dinosaurs were known from Triassic sediments; consequently it had been supposed that these dinosaurs appeared only at the beginning of Jurassic time. Recently, however, the bones of Triassic ornithischian dinosaurs have been found on several continents. The characters of the first ornithischians

FABROSAURUS

are well displayed in a little ornithopod, *Fabrosaurus,* discovered in the upper Triassic beds of South Africa.

Fabrosaurus is a very small dinosaur, no more than three feet in length. Thus it is much smaller than *Coelophysis,* the upper Triassic saurischian dinosaur, described on page 22. As is typical of primitive dinosaurs, *Fabrosaurus* walked and ran on long, slender hind limbs. The fore limbs are quite small and obviously could not have been used for locomotion. The body is slender; the tail is long and served as a counterbalance to the body. The neck is rather short. The small skull is lightly constructed with openings for large eyes.

The teeth of *Fabrosaurus* are especially interesting. The front teeth in the skull are sharp and pointed, but the teeth on the sides of the skull and in the lower jaws are of triangular shape, with numerous small denticles, something like the teeth of a saw, along the cutting edges. And there are no teeth in the front of the lower jaws, but rather a single beak-shaped bone, the predentary bone.

Such an arrangement is quite clearly for nipping and chewing plants. So from the very beginning the ornithischian dinosaurs were plant-eaters. None were carnivorous.

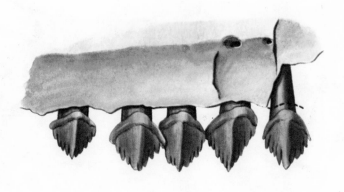

½ inch

1 centimeter

Primitive Ornithopods

It is not uncommon to find primitive animals and plants persisting through the ages so that they live beside their great grandchildren many times removed. *Hypsilophodon,* although a primitive ornithischian dinosaur, is found in rocks of Cretaceous age in England, contemporaneous

HYPSILOPHODON

with many highly specialized and quite varied ornithischians.

Hypsilophodon is no more than four or five feet in length, and is similar to its predecessor, *Fabrosaurus*, in that the hind limbs are long and the fore limbs short, showing that this dinosaur held the body in a semi-erect position. The elongated feet of *Hypsilophodon* are flexible, so it seems probable that this little dinosaur was able to bound along at great speed. Thus it could escape from its enemies.

A few teeth are present in the front of the skull, while in the sides of the skull and the lower jaws there are triangular teeth with little denticles along their cutting edges, similar to the teeth of *Fabrosaurus*. There are two rows of small bony armor plates down the middle of the back. These armor plates appear to be a direct inheritance from the Triassic thecodont reptiles, out of which the two orders of dinosaurs and their relatives were descended.

Camptosaurus, on page 2, known from skeletons found in Jurassic and Cretaceous rocks in North America and Europe, indicates very nicely what the primitive ornithischain dinosaurs were like.

This was a small to medium-sized dinosaur; the skeletons range from about six or seven feet to seventeen feet or more in length. Generally speaking, the skeleton is heavier and more robust than is the skeleton of primitive saurischian dinosaurs. The hind feet are broad and the four toes point foward, so that the foot is not so bird-like as it is·in the early theropods. The five fingers are short and stubby, and it seems likely that this dinosaur came down on all four feet frequently. Certainly the hand appears to be more fitted for support than for grasping. The skull is rather long and low. Even in this generalized type of ornithischian dinosaur the jaws lack teeth in front, and are beaklike.

Camptosaurus persisted through a considerable span of geologic time, and we find its remains associated with the fossils of dinosaurs that may very well have been descended from camptosaur ancestors.

IGUANODON

Diverse Ornithopods

On the facing page is Iguanodon, the first dinosaur to be described from adequate fossil remains, the initial discovery of a few teeth having been made in 1822 by the wife of Gideon Mantell, an English geologist and physician. This lucky find fired the imagination and enthusiasm of Dr. Mantell — to such a degree that he abandoned medicine to devote the rest of his life to fossils, especially to *Iguanodon*. Various fossils of *Iguanodon* were found in southern England during subsequent years, and in 1878 a remarkable group of nearly thirty complete skeletons was unearthed in a coal mine at Bernissart, Belgium. Consequently we have abundant and detailed knowledge of this dinosaur.

Iguanodon was in essence an enlarged camptosaur of early Cretaceous age. The skeleton is about twenty-five or thirty feet in length. One of its distinguishing features is the development of the thumb as a large pointed spur, which may have been a potent weapon of defense for this inoffensive plant-eating dinosaur.

Iguanodon and its close relatives were widely distributed during early Cretaceous time. Such dinosaurs have been found not only in England and northern Europe but also in Spitzbergen (about as close to the North Pole as one can go on land today), in northern Africa, in central Asia and in Australia. Close relatives of *Iguanodon* are found in western North America. Obviously the continents inhabited by *Iguanodon* were more closely connected, with much more uniform temperatures than the continents on which we live.

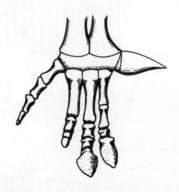

Duck-Billed Dinosaurs

The camptosaurs were ancestors of a varied group of Cretaceous dinosaurs, found in North America and Asia, known as hadrosaurs or duck-billed dinosaurs. These dinosaurs are so named because the front of the skull and the lower jaws are long and flat and broad, and shaped very much like the bill of a duck.

The duck-billed dinosaurs obviously lived along the edges of rivers and lakes, and spent much of their time in the water. It would appear that they shoveled in the mud with their broad bills for food, probably water plants, which they crushed between complex batteries of grinding teeth, located in the sides of the jaws. The teeth in the hadrosaurs are difficult to describe. On each side of the skull and of the lower jaws there are several hundred small, prismatic-like teeth, pressed together in alternating rows. These form four "pavements" of teeth, two on each side opposing each other. But these are pavements in depth, one beneath another — not like the single layer of bricks in an old-fashioned sidewalk. And constantly the rows of teeth were pushing down in the skull and up in the lower jaws, so that as the pavement in use was worn down it was replaced by a new pavement. Consequently there was a constant replacement of teeth, which was necessary, because it would seem that these dinosaurs fed upon tough, fibrous plants.

Fossilized mummies of some of these dinosaurs, in

END VIEW

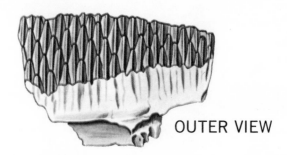

OUTER VIEW

CROWN VIEW

40

which the skin has been petrified, show that they had webs of skin between the toes, as might be expected in a swimming animal.

Anatosaurus, the duck-billed dinosaur commonly known as *Trachodon*, was one of the largest and latest of these ornithischian dinosaurs. It lived in North America at the end of Cretaceous times, along with the giant meat-eater, *Tyrannosaurus*, and with some of the last of the horned dinosaurs. Numerous fossils of this dinosaur have been found, including a number of good skeletons and two excellent petrified mummies.

The skeleton of *Anatosaurus* is about forty feet in length. The skull is very long and flat.

The first dinosaur skeleton to be discovered in North America was that of a duck-billed dinosaur, *Hadrosaurus*, excavated in 1856 at Haddonfield, New Jersey, near Philadelphia. *Hadrosaurus* is very closely related to *Anatosaurus*.

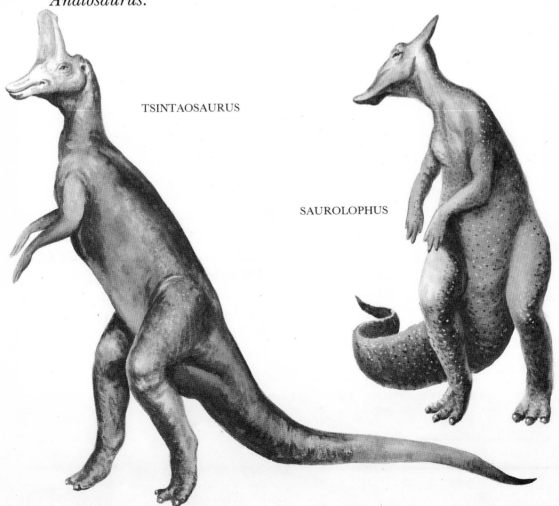

TSINTAOSAURUS

SAUROLOPHUS

PARASAUROLOPHUS

Crested Duck-Bills

Many of the duck-billed dinosaurs have variously shaped crests, on the tops of their skulls. In some of these dinosaurs the crests are formed of solid bone, but in others the crests are hollow and contain complicated loops of the nasal passage.

What was the purpose of this specialization? It has been argued that the skull crests formed accessory reservoirs for the storage of air. But the volume of air that might have been stored in one of these crests is so small as compared with the capacity of the lungs that the use of the crest as an air storage chamber may be questioned. A more recent theory, supported by good evidence, suggests that these crests were lined with mucous membrane, thus affording the crested hadrosaurs a keen sense of smell.

Parasaurolophus, pictured above, and *Corythosaurus,* on the right, are found in the Cretaceous rocks of Alberta.

CORYTHOSAURUS

The Pachycephalosaurs

One suborder of ornithischian dinosaurs is known as the Pachycephalosauria; *pachy* = thick, *cephalos* = head, *sauria* = reptile. As the name indicates, the top of the skull is thickened, to form a large, heavy dome above the brain. These dinosaurs seemingly developed from ornithopod ancestors, and like the ornithopods they show specializations in the skeleton for walking on strong hind limbs. There were various kinds of pachycephalosaurs, some

quite small, others very large, living in western North America and Mongolia during late Cretaceous time.

    Pachycephalosaurus is one of the largest and last of the pachycephalosaurs. This dinosaur shows not only the thick-domed skull, so typical of the pachycephalosaurs, but also a bizarre arrangement of spikes and bumps on the face and on the back of the skull. Why should any dinosaur need nine inches of dense bone above the brain, as is the case in *Pachycephalosaurus*? It has been suggested that the head was used as a sort of battering ram, for butting adversaries.

STEGOCERAS

Stegosaurians

The stegosaurs or plated dinosaurs were typical of the Jurassic period, although some of them persisted briefly into early Cretaceous time. One of the early stegosaurs is *Scelidosaurus*, from the Lower Jurassic rocks of England. This dinosaur is far more advanced in its specializations than are the camptosaurs, described on page 47, which did not appear in the fossil record until late Jurassic times.

STEGOSAURUS

The skeleton of this dinosaur is about twelve feet in length. It is characterized by a completely four-footed pose, a distinct advance beyond the primitive stage of walking on the hind limbs so well displayed in the camptosaur skeleton. The body of *Scelidosaurus* was protected by rows of bony plates that covered the back.

Stegosaurus, so characteristic of the upper Jurassic rocks of western North America, is one of the last and most highly developed of the plated dinosaurs. The skeleton is about twenty feet in length. The skull is very much like the skull of a camptosaur, and is extremely small for an animal as large as *Stegosaurus.* This dinosaur is famous because of the small size of its brain.

It is easy to see that the spikes on the tail of *Stegosaurus* were very useful as weapons of defense, but the purpose of the large, upright bony plates, arranged in two rows down the back, cannot so easily be interpreted, although many people have made suggestions to try to explain the function of these plates.

Close relatives of *Stegosaurus* lived in Europe and in Africa during late Cretaceous time. One of these plated dinosaurs, *Kentrosaurus,* from Tanzania in eastern Africa resembles *Stegosaurus* in many ways, but differs in having fewer and smaller plates on the back and more spikes on the tail.

SCELIDOSAURUS

POLACANTHUS

Armored Dinosaurs

The stegosaurians, so successful during the Jurassic period, became extinct soon after the beginning of Cretaceous times, and their place was taken by the armored dinosaurs, ornithischians in which the body was efficiently protected by bony scutes beneath the skin.

Polacanthus, shown above, one of the early armored dinosaurs, was found in England in sediments of early Cretaceous age. The general form of this dinosaur, the skeleton of which is about fifteen feet in length, is not unlike that of the earlier plated dinosaurs. *Polacanthus* was a dinosaur that walked on four stout legs, with the hips elevated in relation to the shoulders.

The body of *Polacanthus* is covered with a pattern of bony armor plates (in life covered with horny material), and these plates are united to form a broad shield over the hip region. There are large, paired spines along the middle of the back, and a row of spines down the tail. *Polacanthus* would have been a very thorny mouthful for any meat-eating dinosaur that might have been so bold as to attack it.

48

Ankylosaurus and its close relatives that lived during late Cretaceous times in North America and Asia, were well equipped to inhabit environments where giant carnivorous dinosaurs were constantly on the prowl. *Ankylosaurus* about twenty feet in length, was largely covered with a heavy armor of articulating bony plates, arranged in patterns over the body. Even the top and the sides of the skull were protected. Only the belly was unprotected by armor, and it seems likely that when this dinosaur was threatened or attacked, it would have flattened itself close to the ground, to be as invulnerable as possible.

The skeleton of *Ankylosaurus* is remarkable for having a great mass of dense bone on the end of the tail. Thus the tail was a powerful and heavy club that could be swung with bone-crushing effect against any dinosaur that ventured near. *Ankylosaurus* can be looked at as a sort of "reptilian tank."

This robust, heavily armored dinosaur has exceedingly minute, weak teeth, an indication that it probably fed upon soft vegetation.

ANKYLOSAURUS

Ceratopsian Ancestors

In the Cretaceous sediments of Mongolia are found two small dinosaurs showing us the first stages of an evolutionary line that led to the great horned dinosaurs or ceratopsians of North America and eastern Asia.

Psittacosaurus is an ornithischian no more than four or five feet in length. The skeleton of this dinosaur is of a generalized ornithischian type, with long, strong hind legs and small front limbs, but the skull is rather large and deep, and its front part is narrow, so that it resembles the beak of a parrot. The teeth in the sides of the skull and lower jaws are small, with sharp edges, evidently for slicing plant food.

Protoceratops, on the next page, is six or eight feet in length, and it shows many specializations beyond *Psittacosaurus*. *Protoceratops*, even though small in the world of dinosaurs, was a four-footed reptile with large and rather broad feet for good support. The skull in *Protoceratops* is enormous in comparison with the size of the body, the length of the head being almost one third of the total length.

The development of the *Protoceratops* head to such great size was brought about by a great expansion of certain bones on the back of the skull to form a widely flaring frill, extending back over the neck and the shoulders. This

PSITTACOSAURUS

PROTOCERATOPS

frill served for the attachment of powerful jaw and neck muscles. Secondarily it probably protected the neck — an area vulnerable to the attacks of predators. In the largest skulls of *Protoceratops,* presumably those of old male animals, the nasal bone is enlarged so that its upper surface rises to a small point. This is the beginning of a nasal horn, so prominent in the great horned dinosaurs.

Nests of eggs have been found with skeletons of *Protoceratops,* and specimens of various sizes show the development of this dinosaur from the newly hatched baby to the adult animal.

A small ceratopsian, *Leptoceratops,* is found in the upper Cretaceous beds of Alberta. Although *Leptoceratops* was one of the later ceratopsians, living alongside giant horned dinosaurs, it retains many primitive characters that relate it to *Protoceratops.* Indeed, in some respects it is even more primitive than *Protoceratops;* it is smaller and the frill on the skull is less developed than in the Mongolian dinosaur.

Horned Dinosaurs

The giant horned dinosaurs evolved in North America during late Cretaceous times, essentially by enlargements of the structural form established in *Protoceratops,* with elaborations of the skull. The skeleton in all of these dinosaurs is strong, with stout limbs and a comparatively short tail. In all of them the skull is of an enormous size, and is generally about a third of the total length. Since the horned dinosaurs range from eighteen to twenty-four feet or so in length, the skulls are commonly six or seven feet long. The differences between them are largely in the pattern of the horns and the development of the frill. Horns may be large or small and frills may be long or short.

Monoclonius is a ceratopsian with a large horn on the nose. This dinosaur and its relatives, some of which are shown on the next page, may very well be compared with rhinoceroses in the modern world. They defended themselves against attacks from other dinosaurs by fighting back, and must have been formidable reptiles. The great horned skull, backed up by a powerfully muscled body weighing several tons, had a thrust of terrifying force. Evidently the ceratopsians were very successful dinosaurs, and the numbers of their bones indicate that they may have roamed across North America in great herds at the end of the Cretaceous period.

MONOCLONIUS

Skull and Horn Evolution

Here are seen some of the patterns of skull and horn evolution among the ceratopsian dinosaurs of North America.

Triceratops, the last of the ceratopsians, has large horns and a rather short frill.

Pentaceratops has a very long frill, the horns above the eyes are large, the nasal horn is small, and there is an extra set of spikes formed by the jugal bones, on each side of the skull.

Pachyrhinosaurus is a strange ceratopsian that lacks horns, but rather has a large, rough boss or thickened plate covering much of the top of the skull.

Styracosaurus has a profusion of horns and spikes; a large horn on the nose, small horns above the eyes, and long spikes around the edge of the frill.

Chasmosaurus is a rather small ceratopsian, with well-developed horns above the eyes and an almost equally large horn on the nose.

EXTINCTION OF THE DINOSAURS

The dinosaurs, literally the rulers of the earth for more than 100 million years of Mesozoic history, became extinct at the close of the Cretaceous period. These eminently successful reptiles roamed the continents in great numbers and variety up to the very end of Cretaceous times, when they disappeared from the earth within a comparatively short time. Why should this have happened? Why should all the dinosaurs have become extinct? Why did not some of them live on into later geologic ages?

These questions are hard to answer, and in the present stage of our knowledge we can do little more than guess at the causes of dinosaurian extinction. It seems evident that the world changed, and the dinosaurs were unable to change with it. But this general statement leaves much to be explained.

Are any explanations possible? Many have been offered, but none is completely satisfactory.

Did some world-wide catastrophe overwhelm the dinosaurs? If so, why did not certain other contemporaries of the dinosaurs become extinct? Why did the crocodilians, close cousins of the dinosaurs, survive the end of Cretaceous time, to flourish until the present day?

It has been suggested that tiny Cretaceous mammals may have contributed to the extinction of the dinosaurs by eating their eggs. This appears to be an unlikely explanation for the disappearance of such numerous and varied reptiles as the dinosaurs.

It has recently been observed that the fossil eggs of late Cretaceous dinosaurs, found in southern France, have very thin shells. Might there have been some natural factor causing failures in reproduction, parallel to the decrease of certain modern birds, such as the osprey and the pelican, resulting from contamination by DDT?

Perhaps the disappearance of the dinosaurs may be linked with changes in climates, which brought about changes in the vegetation of the world. Revolutions like these in the environment might very well have contributed to the demise of the dinosaurs. Yet we know that climatic changes between Cretaceous times and subsequent ages were slow, and we know that the major changes in the vegetation of the earth took place well before the end of the Cretaceous period. Why, then, did not the dinosaurs adjust themselves to these changes?

One last word. Extinction is one of the important aspects of life on the earth, as is the origin of species. Without extinction there could be no evolutionary progress; life would quickly become static. Old forms of life constantly disappear, under pressure from vigorous new animals and plants which are arising, to multiply and to displace many of their forebears. So it was that the dinosaurs, having occupied the continents for more than a hundred million years (for which reason they may be considered as among the most successful of all animals) finally gave way to the warm-blooded mammals — the modern rulers of the world.

DISTRIBUTION OF THE DINOSAURS

The remains of dinosaurs have been found at many localities throughout the world, the most important ones of which are indicated on this map by dots. These discoveries prove that the dinosaurs were widely distributed across the continents during Mesozoic times. Moreover the occurrences of dinosaurs around the world indicate that there must have been good land connections between the Mesozoic continents, along which the dinosaurs could wander from one land mass to another.

DINOSAURS AND ANCIENT CONTINENTS

The prevalence of dinosaurs throughout the Mesozoic world is made much more comprehensible than otherwise it would be if dinosaurian distributions are viewed in light of the theory of Continental Drift. According to this theory (and with each passing year more evidence accumulates in the fields of geology, geophysics, paleontology and biology, to strengthen the theory) the continents formed a great integrated land mass during late Paleozoic time. This land, known as Pangaea, consisted of two supercontinents, Laurasia in the northern hemisphere and Gondwanaland in the southern hemisphere.

At the close of Triassic time, when early dinosaurs inhabited the lands, Pangaea was beginning to break apart, as seen in the accompanying map. Yet even so, the land masses were so closely in contact that dinosaurs readily moved from one region to another, as is revealed by discoveries of their fossils.

During Jurassic and Cretaceous time the break-up of Pangaea continued. Laurasia became separated from

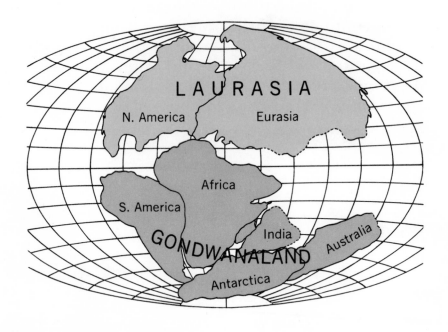

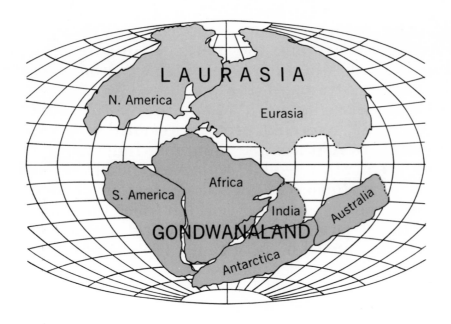

Gondwanaland, yet even so the two supercontinents remained as generally continuous land masses, as shown by the Jurassic map, thus facilitating the wanderings of dinosaurs back and forth. By late Cretaceous time as seen in the map, below, the aspects of our modern continents were

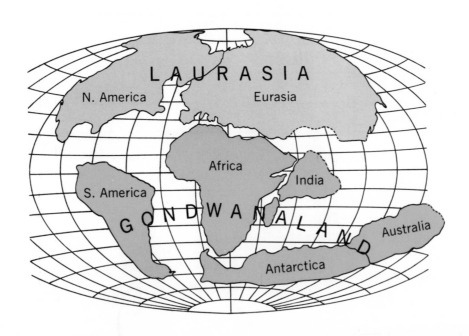

becoming apparent. South America was drifting away from Africa, opening the South Atlantic ocean, and likewise North America was rotating away from the western bulge of Africa and from southern Europe, opening the lower part of the North Atlantic ocean. Antarctica and Australia, still connected, probably retained some contact with southern Africa, while peninsular India was moving north, eventually to collide with Asia, thereby wrinkling up the great Himalaya Range along the zone of collision.

Such was the changing world in which the dinosaurs lived. It was largely a connected world and a tropical world, well suited for the gigantic reptiles which for so long ruled those ancient lands.

Today we find the fossil remains of these ancient reptilian rulers, widely dispersed from their former close associations by the inexorable drifting of the continents.

Period		Saurischians	Ornithischians
CRETACEOUS	Upper		
	Lower		
JURASSIC	Upper		
	Middle		
	Lower		
TRIASSIC	Upper		

COMPARATIVE ABUNDANCE OF DINOSAURS
IN THE MESOZOIC ERA

TEMPERATURE FLUCTUATION IN REPTILES

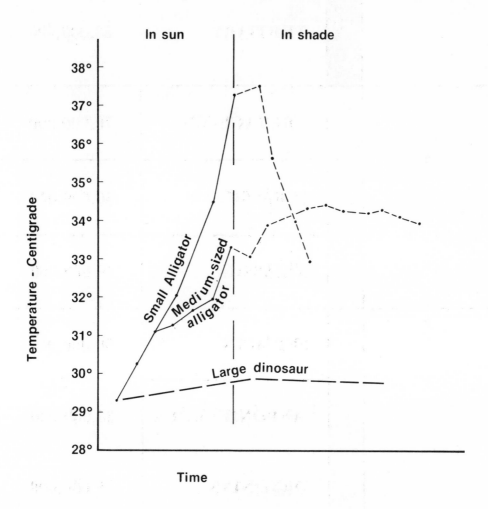

When a small alligator, weighing about 10 pounds, was placed in the Florida sunshine, its body temperature rose rapidly; when it was removed to the shade the temperature fell rapidly.

When a medium-sized alligator, weighing about 30 pounds, was first exposed to the sun and then to the shade, the rise and fall of the body temperature was much slower.

It can be presumed that in a large dinosaur the rise and fall of body temperature would be very slow—thus giving the dinosaur some of the advantages of a warm-blooded animal.

ERAS	PERIODS	DURATION IN YF
CENOZOIC	QUATERNARY	2,000,000
	TERTIARY	63,000,000
MESOZOIC	CRETACEOUS	70,000,000
	JURASSIC	50,000,000
	TRIASSIC	40,000,000
PALEOZOIC	PERMIAN	50,000,000
	CARBONIFEROUS	65,000,000
	DEVONIAN	55,000,000
	SILURIAN	40,000,000
	ORDOVICIAN	65,000,000
	CAMBRIAN	100,000,000
ARCHAEOZOIC PROTEROZOIC		

DOMINANT LIFE	CHARACTERISTIC LIFE
MAN	
MAMMALS	
REPTILES	
AMPHIBIANS	
FISHES	
INVERTEBRATES	
BEGINNING OF LIFE	

PRONOUNCING GUIDE

ALLOSAURUS
(al-o-SAWR-us)
ANATOSAURUS
(an-AT-o-sawr-us)
ANCHISAURUS
(AN-ki-sawr-us)
ANKYLOSAURIA
(an-KYL-o-sawr-e-a)
ANKYLOSAURUS
(an-KYL-o-sawr-us)
BRACHIOSAURUS
(brak-e-o-SAWR-us)
BRONTOSAURUS
(BRON-toe-sawr-us)
CAMPTOSAURUS
(camp-toe-SAWR-us)
CARNOSAURIA
(carn-o-SAWR-e-a)
CERATOPSIA
(cer-a-TOPS-e-a)
CERATOSAURUS
(cer-AT-o-sawr-us)
CHASMOSAURUS
(KAS-mo-sawr-us)
COELOPHYSIS
(seal-o-FI-sis)
COELUROSAURIA
(seal-ur-o-SAWR-e-a)
COMPSOGNATHUS
(comp-sog-NATH-us)

CORYTHOSAURUS
(cor-ITH-o-sawr-us)
DEINONYCHOSAURIA
(dine-o-nyk-o-SAWR-e-a)
DEINOCHEIRUS
(dine-o-KIRE-us)
DEINONYCHUS
(dine-o-NYK-us)
DIPLODOCUS
(dip-LOD-o-cus)
FABROSAURUS
(FAB-ro-sawr-us)
GORGOSAURUS
(GORG-o-sawr-us)
HADROSAURUS
(HAD-ro-sawr-us)
HERRERASAURUS
(her-rar-a-SAWR-us)
HYPSELOSAURUS
(hip-sel-o-SAWR-us)
HYPSILOPHODON
(hip-si-LOF-o-don)
IGUANODON
(i-GWAN-o-don)
KENTROSAURUS
(KEN-tro-sawr-us)
LEPTOCERATOPS
(lep-toe-CER-a-tops)
LUFENGOSAURUS
(lu-feng-o-SAWR-us)

MEGALOSAURUS
(meg-al-o-SAWR-us)
MONOCLONIUS
(mon-o-KLON-e-us)
ORNITHISCHIA
(orn-ith-ISK-e-a)
ORNITHOLESTES
(orn-i-tho-LEST-es)
ORNITHOMIMUS
(orn-i-tho-MIME-us)
ORNITHOPODA
(orn-ith-OP-o-da)
PACHYCEPHALOSAURIA
(pak-e-SEF-al-o-sawr-e-a)
PACHYCEPHALOSAURUS
(pak-e-SEF-al-o-sawr-us)
PACHYRHINOSAURUS
(pak-e-RINE-o-sawr-us)
PARASAUROLOPHUS
(pear-a-sawr-OL-o-fus)
PENTACERATOPS
(pen-ta-SER-a-tops)
PLATEOSAURAVUS
(plat-e-o-sawr-AV-us)
PLATEOSAURUS
(plat-e-o-SAWR-us)
POLACANTHUS
(pole-a-KAN-thus)
PROTOCERATOPS
(pro-toe-SER-a-tops)
PSITTACOSAURUS
(sit-a-ko-SAWR-us)

SAURISCHIA
(sawr-ISS-ke-a)
SAUROLOPHUS
(sawr-OL-o-fus)
SAUROPODA
(sawr-O-po-da)
SCELIDOSAURUS
(skel-ID-o-sawr-us)
STEGOSAURIA
(steg-o-SAWR-e-a)
STEGOSAURUS
(STEG-o-sawr-us)
STYRACOSAURUS
(sty-RAK-o-sawr-us)
SYNTARSUS
(sin-TAR-sus)
TARBOSAURUS
(TAR-bo-sawr-us)
THECODONT
(THE-ko-dont)
THEROPODA
(ther-O-po-da)
TRACHODON
(TRAK-o-don)
TRICERATOPS
(tri-SER-a-tops)
TSINTAOSAURUS
(tsin-TA-o-sawr-us)
TYRANNOSAURUS
(tie-ran-o-SAWR-us)

INDEX